A Homeowner's Guide to Claim Approval:

FOR MAXIMIZING YOUR SETTLEMENT

By M. Wonders

ISBN 979-8-89496-264-1

9 798894 962641

Published by

Staten House

Staten House

Acknowledgment

First and foremost, this book, *A Homeowner's Guide to Claim Approval,* would not have been possible without the sincere consideration of everyone involved in aiding this project through to fruition. Therefore, this is for you all…

They say, "persistence is key." It seems I was taught that early in my pre-teen era, without realizing it. However, I do recall moments from my school teachers, friends, and family, when they would express that I have a gift in literature and being creative. Back then, before, advance smart phones, and home computers, there was sincere appreciation for imagination and what it can do in books. I prefer motion-media, but if a book could hold my attention… my mind had no limits and I would absorb the author's techniques used to capture me, and apply it to fictional stories, song writing, love letters, and poetry, etc. My writing hobby became distracted by life, of course, but I never forgot the growth & develop because of my journey.

Fast forward to now. Life still is the best teacher. I've learned and apply the "Golden Rule," treat others as you want to be treated, and that one must give in order to get. For these principles, I thank Jesus Christ, my Shepard and Savior. For my values, I thank my migrant mother (RIP) and father, who instilled into me perfection is not possible, but it is the goal. My credentials include being a license licensed Claims Adjuster. I'm also blessed to have two beautiful sisters, whom I love dearly, as if they were my own. My love for family, encourages me to use my God-given gifts for good, for all.

True friends… how many of us have them? I don't have many, but I do have a circle of trustees, and everyone contributed to this day in one way or another. I'd like to thank Diana C., my life-long friend. She is woman of great insight and ambition, who knows no limit. Her versatile entrepreneurship accomplishments and love for people is extremely rare. Thank you for timely encouragement to get back up. I'd like to thank Kimberly B. for her dedication to her life's calling and focus. She has done everything under the sun, and is the first person I personally know, to publish her 1st book, as a Life Coach - A big deal for her (and me)! That was the moment I had a flashback to my teenage era, envisioning, what if I did start a book. Now, I can join her level of accomplishments! She truly has a beautiful spirit. Let's not forget my brother from another mother, "Sleeping Dragon." This guy needs a book about him-self! We talk all the time. He knows that he means a lot to me. Thank you for everything. You sir, are the G.O.A.T. To all the Claim Adjusters who peer-reviewed this book for accuracy, thank you – thank you – thank you! The immense experience, on the field and behind the desk, provides an invaluable perspective.

Lastly, I must give a solid thank you to the formal sources who aided to this book as well. Thanks to ConsumerReports.com, EPA.gov, and NAIC.org for allowing homeowners to be well informed as a consumer. Without these thoroughly researched consumer sources, life would be more chaotic. As for Marketing Abstract Advertising, LLC, this entire book would not have been possible without the hard work, collaboration, wise counsel, and professionalism provided. Thank you all sincerely.

Unpacking The Reader Disclosure

This book, *A Homeowner's Guide to Claim Approval,* ...

1. Unless indicated, is comprised of filtered homeowners' insurance claim information from the world wide web (internet), which requires the audience or the beholder of this publication, to do their own research.

2. ConsumerReports.com, NAIC.org, and EPA.gov are referenced with permission.

3. Has been authored by a licensed Claim Adjuster and peer-reviewed by a combined 50+ years of field and desk experience by licensed Claim Adjusters.

4. Is a "how-to," "faith-based," "self-help," "Do-It-Yourself (DIY)" book for homeowners seeking an easy-to-read insurance claim guide.

5. Does not guarantee an approved property claim settlement by a property insurance carrier.

6. Is meant to serve those who do not have the budget for professional claim processing assistance, but can do it themselves with an insurance claim guide.

7. Is meant to simplify the complexity of property claims into an easy-to-read guide for first-time homeowners, seasoned homeowners, and multiple property owners.

Advocating For Homeowners

Consumer awareness, in regards to Homeowners, is crucial for informed decision-making and protection against exploitation! Below are my reasons why I believe **HOMEOWNER AWARENESS IS IMPORTANT**:

> **Proverbs**
>
> **24: 3 - 4**
>
> " *By wisdom a house is built, and through understanding it is established; through knowledge its rooms are filled with rare and beautiful treasures.*

1. **Empowerment**: Providing knowledge and tools to assert homeowners' rights, in the marketplace, **making choices that align with their preferences and values**.

2. **Maximum Satisfaction at the Best Price**: When consumers are aware of product quality and pricing, they can **choose the best value for their money to achieve maximum satisfaction by making informed decisions**.

3. **Protection from Exploitation**: Awareness acts as a shield against exploitation, **ensuring fair transactions and safeguarding consumer interests**.

4. **Market Accountability**: Well-informed consumers demand fair treatment and value for their money, **promoting transparency and ethical practices in a marketplace where businesses are held accountable for their actions**.

5. **Reduction of Fraud:** Awareness about scams, fraudulent schemes, and unethical practices helps consumers **avoid falling victim to fraud and protect themselves from financial losses and deceptive marketing tactics**.

Table of Contents

CHAPTER 1

Homeowners' Insurance 101

Chapter 1: Homeowners Insurance 101

Homeowners' insurance coverage is an important purchase for first-time, seasoned, and multiple property owners. According to the National Association of Insurance Commissioners (NAIC), homeowners' insurance is purchased either to protect the homeowners' assets or to satisfy your mortgage lender.

Understanding the basics of homeowners insurance is crucial for homeowners. Homeowners insurance provides financial protection for your home and belongings. It covers losses due to events like plumbing leaks, wind, fire, theft, vandalism, or natural disasters. Familiarize yourself with the claim process, premiums, and deductibles by annually reviewing your policy to stay informed about coverage limits and exclusions. Being well-informed helps you protect your investment effectively.

Insurance Claim Roles

Let's explore the significance of each licensed professional's role in the property insurance industry during the claims process. These individuals work together to ensure fair compensation for policyholders after unexpected events.

Let's delve into the roles and significance of each term in the property insurance industry:

1. **Insurance Carriers:**
   - ➤ **Purpose**: Insurance carriers, also known as insurance companies, are the backbone of the insurance industry. They underwrite and provide coverage for various risks.

   - ➤ **Reason**: Without carriers, insurance as we know it would not exist. They assess risks, set premium rates, and pay out claims when losses occur.

2. **Insurance Agent:**
    - ➤ **Purpose**: Insurance agents sell, service, and negotiate insurance policies on behalf of carriers. They connect customers with suitable coverage.

    - ➤ **Reason**: Agents act as intermediaries, helping clients understand their options and find the right policies for their needs.

3. **Field Adjuster:**
    - ➤ **Purpose**: Field adjusters investigate insurance claims by visiting the site of incidents (e.g., property damage). They assess damage firsthand.

    - ➤ **Reason**: Their assessments determine how much the carrier should pay for the loss, ensuring fair compensation.

4. **Desk Adjuster:**
    - ➤ **Purpose**: Unlike field adjusters, desk adjusters handle claims from an office setting. They review information provided by field adjusters or claimants.

    - ➤ **Reason**: Desk adjusters make decisions on claims, considering policy terms, coverage limits, and evidence.

5. **Public Adjuster:**
    - ➤ **Purpose**: Public adjusters work independently from carriers. They assist policyholders in filing claims and negotiate fair settlements.

    - ➤ **Reason**: They represent the insured's interests, ensuring a balanced claims process and maximizing compensation.

6. **Claims Attorney:**
    - ➤ **Purpose**: Claims attorneys specialize in handling insurance disputes. They may represent either policyholders or insurers.

    - ➤ **Reason**: Attorneys navigate legal complexities, ensuring fair outcomes and resolving disagreements over claim payouts.

Insurance Industry Premiums

Numerous elements influence the insurance premium you incur, such as the choice of insurance provider. Additionally, the choices you make regarding the extent of insurance coverage you purchase play a role in determining your premium costs. Some of the other things that are likely to affect your premium are:

➤ **Deductible**: Choosing a higher deductible can reduce your monthly insurance costs. However, it also means you'll face greater out-of-pocket expenses when making a claim.

➤ **Limits of Coverage**: The coverage limits you set for your dwelling and personal property have a direct impact on your insurance rates. The more expensive it is to reconstruct your home, the more extensive coverage you'll require.

➤ **Home's Age**: Typically, an older home is more prone to issues, increasing the likelihood of filing a claim. This can result in a higher cost for repairs or replacements, which often translates to increased insurance premiums, independent of your coverage limits.

➤ **Location of Home**: Homes situated in densely populated regions or areas prone to frequent weather events tend to have higher insurance premiums.

A Homeowner's Coverage Quote

When you get quotes, it's crucial that you ask for the same coverages and limits and give the same information to each agent or company.

Many insurance providers offer reduced rates for bundling your home and auto insurance policies. When inquiring About Discounts: It's important to consult with your insurance agent regarding potential discounts. Additionally, taking proactive measures to safeguard your home against disaster, such as installing storm shutters, modernizing electrical or plumbing systems, replacing an old roof, or implementing security measures like burglar alarms, etc., can also lead to discounts. Also, be sure to find out how much your premium will change if you choose different deductibles.

Premium Increase Again?!

Insurance companies have experienced reduced earnings due to the rise in natural disasters. Consequently, several insurers have withdrawn from the Florida homeowner market due to substantial claim payouts. Homeowners who have recently filed claims may observe higher insurance premiums. Similar to auto insurance, homeowners' insurance providers often impose a surcharge for three years following a claim.

In most states, regulators have to approve insurers' plans to raise their premiums, and those rate increases don't always get approved. Here are some reasons why insurance premiums increase:

> **Impact of Natural Disasters**: The cost of home construction has been influenced by major natural disasters in recent times. Notably, the repercussions of Hurricane Ian, which ranks among the most expensive storms in the history of the United States.

> **Claim Frequency Increase**: In regions that have endured significant disasters over several years, insurance companies have received authorization from state regulators to increase premiums. This adjustment compensates for the accumulated claims and elevated risk. Such rate hikes can impact all homeowners within the area, including those who have never submitted a claim. Occasionally, a surge in claims can lead insurers to withdraw from a market or cancel policies, compelling affected homeowners to seek new insurance providers.

> **Litigation and Fraud**: The expenses associated with litigation are being factored into the rate adjustments submitted by insurers to state regulatory bodies, which in turn affects the pricing of insurance policies.

For more information about Insurance Premiums, visit: www.consumerreports.org

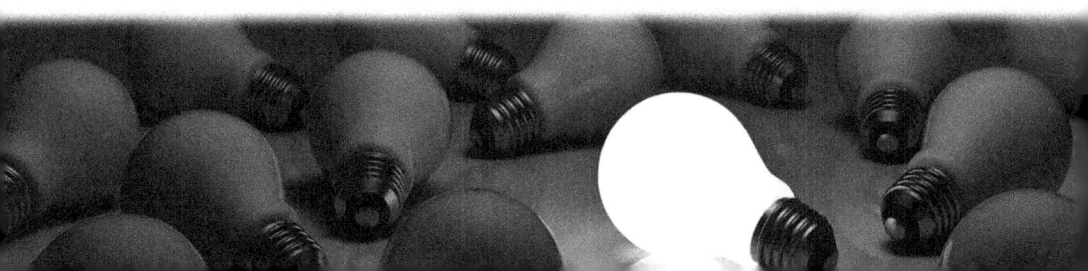

Lower Homeowner's Insurance Premiums

Homeowners have several avenues to decrease their insurance expenses. By choosing a higher deductible, the monthly insurance rates can be minimized. If that is the case, just be prepared to cover this amount if a claim arises. Upgrade plumbing system, replace roof, installing a robust security system, and opting to handle small repairs less than your deductible can contribute to premium reductions.

Proactively seeking out discounts, especially for home improvements or policy bundles, is advisable. A solid credit score can positively affect insurance rates, so it's worth improving it. It's wise to shop around for competitive insurance quotes and to reassess your coverage to ensure it aligns with your actual needs. Taking preventative measures against natural disasters and consolidating insurance policies under one provider can also lead to cost savings. By following these strategies, homeowners can not only cut down on insurance costs but also bolster their home's defenses. Be sure to speak with your sales agent or carrier for available discounts.

Do I Need Additional Coverage?

Maybe you do... Maybe you don't. If your primary insurance does not provide coverage for a peril that you want covered, the homeowner can purchase Supplemental Coverage to protect against specific risks. The additional coverages can either be an Endorsement or an additional Homeowners Insurance policy.

➤ **Endorsements**: An adjustment to your current homeowners insurance by adding, changing, or excluding certain aspects of the coverage. They are integrated into your main policy to cater to specific needs, like covering high-value items or specific risks.

➤ **Supplemental Insurance Policies**: Completely separate contracts that offer additional coverage for risks not included in your standard policy, such as natural disasters. These policies stand alone with their own set of terms and premiums.

When a homeowner has both a private insurance policy and a federal insurance program like the National Flood Insurance Program (NFIP), there's a system in place to determine which insurance pays first, known as **Coordination of Benefits** (COB). This system is designed to prevent double payment or insurance benefits overlap for the same claim.

For example, if a homeowner has both NFIP flood insurance and a private homeowners policy, and their home sustains flood damage, the NFIP policy would typically be the primary payer for flood-related claims. The private insurance might then cover additional living expenses or other costs not covered by the NFIP policy. Here's how it typically works:

1. The primary payer (which could be either the private insurance or the federal program, depending on the situation) pays up to the limits of its coverage first.
2. Then, the secondary payer covers some or all of the remaining costs, up to the coverage limits of its policy.
3. If there are still outstanding costs, the homeowner may be responsible for paying them.

It's important for homeowners to understand their policies and coordinate coverage to ensure they are fully protected and know which insurance will cover a given claim. Homeowners should also communicate with both their private insurance provider and any federal program insurers to understand the specifics of how their policies interact.

Claim History Review

When an insurance carrier processes a new claim, as part of their coverage determination process, a claim history check is always performed. Insurance companies review a homeowner's history of claims to evaluate the risk they present, to prevent fraud, to set appropriate premium rates, and to use comprehensive databases like Comprehensive Loss Underwriting Exchange "CLUE" reports, to see a full history of claims.

Why claim history matters to insurers? When a homeowner files a property claim, insurers look at their past claims to assess how much of a risk they are, to check for any fraudulent patterns, to determine fair pricing for their policy, and to consult databases that track claim histories across different insurance providers. This thorough review helps insurance companies manage their risk and ensure fair policy pricing. Here are some examples why:

1. **Risk Assessment**: Insurance companies evaluate the likelihood of future claims. By checking your claim history, they gauge the risk associated with insuring you. Frequent claims may indicate higher risk.

2. **Fraud Prevention**: Insurers verify the legitimacy of claims. A history of suspicious or fraudulent claims could raise concerns. Detecting fraud helps maintain fair premiums for all policyholders.

3. **Coverage Limits**: Insurers consider your claim history when determining coverage limits. Extensive past claims might affect the maximum amount they'll pay for future losses.

4. **Premium Calculation**: Your claims impact your premium. Frequent claims may lead to higher premiums. Insurers use this data to set fair rates based on risk.

Should I Start A Claim?

Subjectively, 99% of homeowner's *WILL* file a property claim once in their lifetime. The question is not, "Should I?" The question is "How do I?" Ultimately, as the world evolves and climate continues to intensify, sea levels rising, greater risk is forcing businesses and homeowners to adjust and prepare accordingly. Let's explore the pros and cons of filing a homeowners insurance claim versus not filing one.

Submitting a claim offers monetary assistance for restorations or replacements following an insured incident. It alleviates the pressure of bearing the expenses alone, particularly in the face of substantial damages. The assurance that your insurance is there to support you in times of crisis can provide a sense of security, enabling you to concentrate on getting back on your feet without the stress of financial strain. Moreover, if your policy encompasses a certain event, exercising your legal entitlement to file a claim is important, as neglecting to do so might lead to a forfeiture of coverage. Given that every scenario is distinct, it's crucial to ponder over these aspects when determining whether to proceed with a claim.

Before submitting a claim for homeowners insurance, it's important to assess the possible consequences. Initiating a claim can trigger a rise in your premiums, as insurance providers might categorize you as a greater liability, which could inflate the price of subsequent policies. Remember, your deductible must be met prior to the activation of your insurance benefits. If the damage is marginal and approximates the amount of your deductible, pursuing a claim may not be economically justifiable. Insurers keep a record of your claim history; a pattern of frequent claims could affect your ability to secure coverage or even result in policy non-renewal. Consider these elements judiciously in your decision-making process.

Choosing not to file a claim preserves your record as claims-free, which can be beneficial when you're in the market for new insurance or discussing rates. Keeping your claims history clean ensures that your premiums stay consistent, sparing you from possible increases. When it comes to minor repairs, it might be more financially sensible to handle the expenses yourself if the expenses are less than your deductible.

Fortunately, *A Homeowner's Guide to Claim Approval* will explain the entire process to maximize your settlement. Before you report, consult with your agent or representative to discuss your specific loss. See what Consumer Reports says about starting a claim homeowners' Insurance claim.

CHAPTER 2

Understanding
Your Policy

Chapter 2: Understanding Your Policy

There are several types of homeowners insurance policies to choose from, each tailored to different needs. Choose the policy that best suits your home and circumstances. Always consult your policy details and insurer for specific coverage information.

Here are the most common ones:

- ➤ **HO-3 (Standard Policy)**: This is the most common type for single-family homes. It provides broad coverage for your home and belongings, including named perils like fire, theft, and windstorm.

- ➤ **HO-5 (Comprehensive Policy)**: Offers even more comprehensive coverage than HO-3. It covers your home and personal property on an open-perils basis (unless specifically excluded), making it a robust choice.

- ➤ **HO-4 (Renters Insurance)**: Specifically for tenants, it covers personal belongings and liability but not the physical structure of the rented property.

- ➤ **HO-6 (Condo Insurance)**: Designed for condo owners, it covers your personal property, liability, and improvements within your unit.

- ➤ **HO-7 (Mobile or Manufactured Home Insurance)**: If you own a mobile or manufactured home, this policy type provides coverage for your dwelling and belongings.

- ➤ **HO-8 (Older Property Insurance)**: Tailored for older homes that cost more to rebuild than their market value. It considers historical features and unique construction.

Key Components of Property Insurance Policies

Homeowners insurance policies typically include several key components to provide comprehensive coverage. Review the components listed below, choose coverage limits that adequately protect your assets and yourself, and consult with your insurance agent.

1. **Dwelling Coverage:**
   - This core component covers damage to your home and attached structures (such as a porch) due to events like fire, storms, or lightning strikes. It ensures you can repair or replace your main dwelling if unforeseen calamities occur.

2. **Other Structures Coverage:**
   - Standard homeowners' insurance typically covers fences if they are damaged by sudden perils such as storms, fallen trees, or vandalism.
   - This coverage is designed to protect detached structures on your property, including fences, garden sheds, and detached garages.
   - It helps pay for repairs or replacement if your fence sustains damage from covered events (e.g., fire, windstorms, hail, vandalism) unless specifically excluded by your policy. However, coverage pays for repair costs up to the fence's current cash value, not the full replacement value of the original cost. Like cars, fences depreciate in value over time due to wear and tear from being outdoors.

3. **Personal Property Coverage:**
   - This part pays to repair or replace your stolen or damaged belongings, such as furniture, electronics, and clothing. It's typically 50% of Dwelling Coverage Limit.

4. **Additional Living Expenses (ALE) Coverage:**
   - The "loss of use" coverage limit is typically a percentage of your dwelling coverage. For homeowners, it often defaults to 20% of the insured structure value.
   - For example, if your home is insured for $300,000, your loss of use limit would be $60,000.

- ○ **ALE includes three parts:**

  - **Loss of Use**: If your home becomes uninhabitable due to a covered disaster, this coverage helps pay for temporary living expenses (like hotel costs) while your home is being repaired. Depending on your policy, it can pay until your home is fully repaired or you relocate permanently.

  - **Fair Rental Value (loss of rental income)**: Helps recoup lost rental income if you rent out part of your space and your tenant must move out during repairs.

  - **Prohibited Use**: Assists when your home is inaccessible due to nearby damage (even if your home isn't directly damaged).

5. **Liability Protection**: Homeowners insurance can help cover legal costs if someone gets injured on your property or if you accidentally damage someone else's property. The coverage amount usually ranges from $100,000 to $500,000.

Clarifying Coverage Limits

In addition to coverage limits, policies have terms, conditions, and exclusions, you should be aware of. Remember coverage varies based on the policy, provider, and cause of damage. Review your policy and consider additional coverage if needed! Always consult your policy details and insurer for specific coverage information. Let's jump into coverage limits:

COVERAGE LIMITS:

- ➢ **Dwelling Coverage**: Covers your home and <u>attached</u> structures (carports, lanais, pool cage, etc). Pays for damage to your house and to structures attached to your house. This includes damage to fixtures, such as plumbing, electrical wiring, heating and permanently installed air-conditioning systems. It should be enough to fully rebuild your home if necessary.

➢ **Other Structures**: Pays for damage to fences, tool sheds, freestanding garages, guest cottages and other structures <u>not attached</u> to your house. Typically, 10% of dwelling coverage for detached structures (like a garage or shed).

➢ **Personal Property**: Reimburses you for the value of your possessions, including furniture, electronics, appliances and clothing, damaged or lost even when they aren't on your property, such as those at an off-site storage locker or with your child at college. Usually 50% - 70% of dwelling coverage for belongings (furniture, electronics, etc.).

➢ **Loss of Use**: Pays some of your additional living expenses while your home is being repaired. About 20% of dwelling coverage for temporary living expenses during repairs.

➢ **Personal Liability**: Covers your financial loss if you are sued and found legally responsible for injuries or damages to someone else. Typically starts at $100,000 but can be higher.

➢ **Medical Payments**: Pays medical bills for people hurt on your property or hurt by your pets. Minimum limit is $1,000, but higher limits are available.

➢ **Other Coverages**: Identity fraud protection, jewelry coverage, and more.

<u>Clarifying Deductibles</u>

The homeowner's deductible amount is subtracted from the total repair estimate. This is the portion the homeowner is responsible for paying out of pocket before insurance coverage kicks in.

In summary, daily deductibles apply broadly to different types of claims, while hurricane deductibles specifically address damage from hurricanes and windstorms. Consult with your agent or representative to tailor your coverage to your specific needs.

Let's dive into the difference between daily deductibles and hurricane deductibles in homeowners' insurance:

1. **Daily Deductible:**
   - A daily deductible is the standard deductible that applies to various types of claims, not just specific to hurricanes. It's what you're responsible for paying out of pocket before your insurance company covers the rest.

   - Most standard home insurance policies have a daily deductible ranging from $500 to $2,500 for each claim.

   - The daily deductible applies to a wide range of perils, including fire, theft, and water damage.

2. **Hurricane Deductible:**
   - Hurricane deductibles are specific to damage caused by hurricanes or severe windstorms. They are triggered when your home is damaged by wind or rain from a hurricane.

   - Unlike daily deductibles, hurricane deductibles are usually higher and calculated as a percentage of your home's insured value. The percentage typically ranges from 1% to 5% of the dwelling coverage.

   - In some coastal areas with high wind risk, hurricane deductibles can be even higher.

   - Note that flooding caused by a hurricane IS NOT covered by standard home insurance. You'll need a separate flood insurance policy for flood protection.

3. **No deductible for Personal Liability coverage.**

Clarifying Coverage Conditions

Homeowners insurance policies include several conditions clauses that outline important terms and requirements. Review your policy thoroughly to understand these conditions and ensure proper coverage! Here are some common ones:

- ➤ **Exclusions, Acts of God, and Named Perils**:
  - ○ Exclusions specify what events are not covered. Acts of God (natural disasters) like tornadoes and wildfires fall into this category.
  - ○ Named perils refer to specific covered risks (e.g., fire, theft, vandalism).

- ➤ **Limits on Certain Personal Property**:
  - ○ Policies often have limits on coverage for specific items (e.g., jewelry, electronics). Review these limits to ensure adequate protection.

- ➤ **Mortgagee Clause**:
  - ○ This clause addresses the rights and responsibilities of the mortgage lender (mortgagee) regarding insurance coverage on the property.

- ➤ **Coinsurance Clause**:
  - ○ Coinsurance ensures that you maintain adequate coverage relative to your home's value. If your home is vacant for an extended period, this clause may impact coverage. Notify your insurer if your home will be unoccupied.

- ➤ **Appraisal Clause**:
  - ○ The appraisal process resolves disputes over the amount owed on an insured loss. It's an alternative to legal proceedings, aiming for cost-effective resolution.

- ➤ **Limits on Personal Liability Coverage**:
  - ○ Understand the maximum liability coverage provided in case of accidents or injuries on your property.

Conditions (Continued)

After a loss, homeowners have specific post-loss duties outlined in their insurance policies. Fulfilling these duties is crucial to ensure a successful insurance claim process! These duties are essential to ensure a smooth claims process:

➢ **Duty to Provide Prompt Notice**:

   o Notify your insurance company as soon as possible after a loss occurs.

   o Prompt notice allows the insurer to assess the situation, begin the claims process, and take necessary actions to mitigate further damage.

➢ **Duty to Mitigate Damages**:

   o Take immediate and reasonable steps to minimize further harm or loss to the property.

   o Actions include temporary repairs, boarding broken windows, and stopping leaks.

   o Mitigating damages reduces repair costs and demonstrates good faith to the insurer.

➢ **Duty to Permit a Property Inspection**:

   o Allow the insurance company or their representatives to inspect the property.

   o This thorough inspection helps evaluate and document the harm for the claim.

Clarify Coverage Exclusions

Homeowners insurance policies include specific exclusion clauses that outline what is not covered. Here are some common exclusions:

➢ **Flooding**: Damage caused by natural floods, rain, sewer backups, or ground seepage isn't covered.

➤ **<u>Plumbing Systems</u>**: the insurance company may pay for the tear-out and replacement of building items to access the plumbing system, but not necessarily the plumbing itself. <u>It's essential to note that routine maintenance or wear and tear of your plumbing system is not covered by homeowners' insurance.</u>

➤ **<u>Earth Movements</u>**: Earthquakes, land shock waves, volcanic eruptions, landslides, and sinkholes are excluded. However, fire or explosion damage due to earth movement is covered.

➤ **<u>Pest Infestations</u>**: Damage caused by animals (rats, termites, bees, etc.) is generally not covered unless under rare circumstances.

➤ **<u>Wear and Tear or Neglect</u>**: Gradual wear-and-tear, marring, deterioration, and neglect are excluded.

➤ **<u>Power Surges from Utility Companies</u>**: Damage resulting from utility company power surges is typically not covered.

➤ **<u>Home-Based Business Liability</u>**: Liability related to home-based businesses may require separate coverage.

Consult with your agent or representative to tailor your coverage to your specific needs. Remember coverage varies based on the policy, provider, and cause of damage.

Review your policy and consider additional coverage if needed! Always consult your policy details and insurer for specific coverage information.

<u>What About Matching?!?</u>

In summary, Like Kind and Quality (LKQ), in Property Insurance ensures that insured property is restored <u>as closely as possible to its original state</u> to what it was before the loss occurred, considering practical constraints and reasonable standards.

➢ **Definition**: In property insurance policies, the term "**Like, Kind, and Quality**" (LKQ) refers to a condition where the insurer agrees to cover the cost of repairing or replacing a covered loss with property that is **similar to the original** in **composition and quality**.

➢ **Explanation**:

  ○ Suppose you have car insurance, and your new car is involved in an auto accident. If the policy covers the loss, the insurer is legally obligated to pay for repairs using products and parts from the original manufacturer. If that's not possible, they must use materials comparable to the original.

  ○ Similarly, for other types of property (such as a home or business), LKQ ensures that repairs or replacements maintain the same standard as the original.

➢ **Limits to Matching**:

  ○ While LKQ aims for similarity, there are practical limits:

  ○ **Availability**: If the exact original materials or parts are no longer available (e.g., due to discontinuation), the insurer may use the closest available substitutes.

  ○ **Age and Wear**: The replacement may not match exactly if the original property had wear and tear or aging. For example, a new roof may not perfectly match an older one.

  ○ **Upgrades**: If you choose to upgrade during repairs (e.g., opting for a better-quality material), you may need to cover the cost difference.

  ○ **Reasonable Cost**: Insurers won't pay for excessive costs to achieve an exact match if it's not practical or reasonable.

Statute Of Limitations

Timely action is essential to protect your rights as a homeowner! As a homeowner, understanding the statute of limitations is crucial. It refers to the time limit within which you can file a legal claim related to your property. Here are some key points:

- ➤ **Property Damage Claims**: If your home sustains damage due to a storm, fire, or other incidents covered by your insurance policy, you typically have a limited time (usually a few years) to file a claim. After this period, you may lose your right to seek compensation.

- ➤ **Legal Actions**: Suppose you need to take legal action against someone (e.g., a contractor, neighbor, or previous owner) regarding property issues. The statute of limitations determines how long you have to initiate legal proceedings.

- ➤ **State-Specific Rules**: Keep in mind that the statute of limitations varies by state and the type of claim. Consult your local laws or seek legal advice to understand the specific timeframes relevant to your situation.

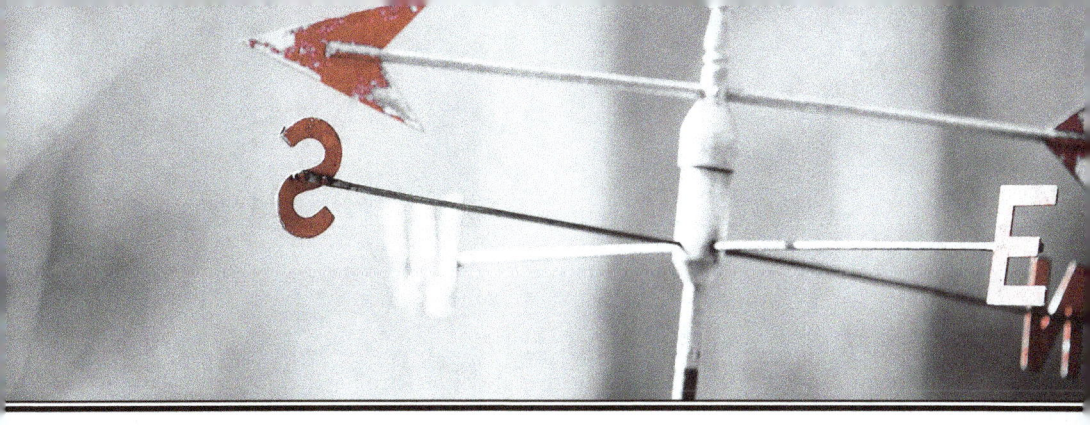

CHAPTER 3

....

Common Peril Claims

Chapter 3: Common Peril Claims

T he most common insurance claims homeowners face include damage from wind and hail, costly fire and lightning incidents, water damage and freezing conditions, a variety of other property damages, and liability issues for injuries or damage to others' property.

Involve the appropriate professionals promptly to assess and estimate repair costs for your specific claim. Here are some common homeowners' insurance claim causes of loss, along with the specific skilled trades needed for repair estimates:

➤ **Structural Damage - Skilled Trade Needed:**

   ○ Engineers - They evaluate the impact on the home's structure and foundation.

➤ **Wind and Hail Damage / Roof Leak - Skilled Trade Needed:**

   ○ Roofing Contractors - They assess roof damage, replace shingles, and repair any structural issues caused by wind or hail.

   ○ Engineers - They evaluate the impact on the home's structure and roof condition.

➤ **Fire and Lightning Damage - Skilled Trade Needed:**

   ○ Fire Restoration Specialists or General Contractors - They evaluate fire-damaged areas, repair structural components, and handle smoke damage restoration.

➤ **Water Damage (Non-Weather Related) - Skilled Trade Needed:**

   ○ Plumbers or Water Damage Restoration Experts - They identify leaks, fix broken pipes, and restore affected areas.

   ○ HVAC Technicians - If heating ventilation, or air conditioning systems are impacted, they estimate repairs.

- **Mold Damages - Skilled Trade Needed:**

  - Mold Remediation Technicians: These experts handle the actual removal of mold. They follow safety protocols, contain affected areas, and use specialized equipment to clean and disinfect.

- **Theft-Related Damage - Skilled Trade Needed:**

  - General Contractors or Carpenters - They repair doors, windows, and other entry points damaged during a break-in.

- **Electrical/Power Surge - Skilled Trade Needed:**

  - Electricians - If electrical systems within the home are affected by the impact, they assess and estimate repairs.

  - Appliance Service Technicians - If appliances are affected, they assess and repair or replace damaged units.

- **Catastrophic Damages - Skilled Trade Needed:**

  - General Contractors - They oversee the entire repair process, assess structural damage, and provide an overall estimate.

- **Bodily Injury Claims - Skilled Trade Needed:**

  - While not directly related to repair estimates, consult an Attorney or Insurance Counselor for legal guidance in these cases.

Plumbing Leak!! Where?!

Address leaks promptly to prevent further damage and costly repairs! Here are some common types of plumbing leaks:

- ➤ **Pipe Leaks Under Sinks**: These occur beneath kitchen or bathroom sinks. They can lead to water damage if not promptly addressed.

- ➤ **Slab Leaks/Foundational Leaks**: These occur within the concrete slab foundation of a building. They can be challenging to detect and may cause structural issues.

- ➤ **Leaks Behind Drywall**: These hidden leaks can occur within walls, often due to damaged pipes or faulty connections.

- ➤ **Toilet Leaks**: Toilet leaks can happen at the base, around the tank, or within the bowl. They may cause water damage or waste leakage.

- ➤ **Water Heater Leaks**: Water heaters can develop leaks, leading to water damage and potential system failure.

- ➤ **HVAC Technicians**: If heating, ventilation, or air conditioning systems are impacted, they estimate repairs.

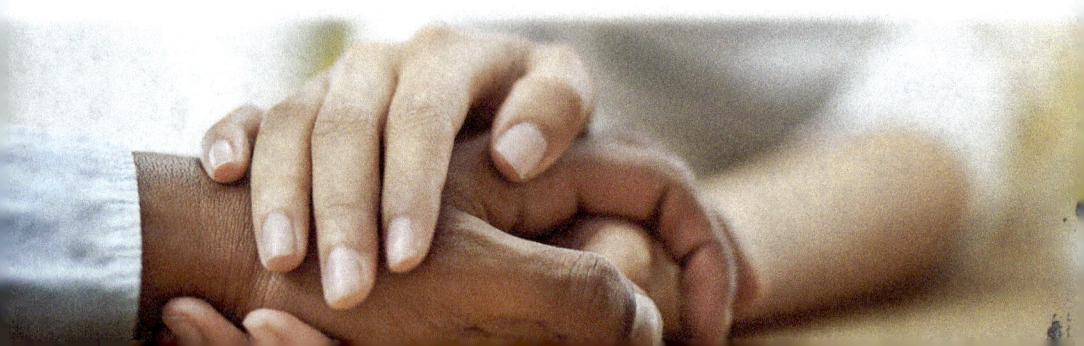

CHAPTER 4

Proactive Measures

Chapter 4: Proactive Measures

As a homeowner, proactive measures play a crucial role in ensuring a smooth insurance claims process. Timely claim submission and effective documentation are critical for homeowners navigating insurance claims. Submitting claims promptly ensures faster access to coverage, while thorough documentation substantiates losses and expedites the process. Visual evidence (photos), receipts, communication records, and home inventories play key roles. Being proactive maximizes the chances of a successful claim settlement.

Timely Claim Submission

Timely and thorough action can make a significant difference in claim approval! Here are **five critical tips** to help you submit homeowners' insurance claims effectively and prevent denials:

- ➤ **Prompt Notification**: Notify your insurer **immediately** after a loss occurs. Understand the **time limits** for filing a claim.

- ➤ **Premium Payments**: Pay your premiums **on time** to maintain active coverage.

- ➤ **Know Your Policy**: Understand what your policy **covers** and **excludes**. Obtain adequate coverage if possible.

- ➤ **Mitigate Damage**: After a loss, take **reasonable steps** to protect your property and **minimize damage**.

- ➤ **Document Everything**: Collect **detailed evidence**, including photographs, receipts, and contractor inspections. File a **thorough itemized claim** with your insurer.

Effective Documentation

When dealing with homeowners insurance claims, proper documentation is crucial to prevent denials and ensure approval. Remember, accurate and comprehensive documentation can significantly impact the success of your homeowner insurance claim. Here are five practical tips for effective documentation:

1. **Collect Evidence:**
   - Gather detailed evidence, including photos and receipts. Take overall and close-up pictures of the damage. Keep records of all communication, noting what information you shared and when. Email communication can create a useful paper trail.

2. **Home Inventory:**
   - Maintain an up-to-date inventory of your belongings. Include descriptions, purchase dates, and estimated values. This inventory streamlines the claims process and provides evidence of your losses.

3. **Police Reports:**
   - If a crime like theft or vandalism occurs, file a police report before contacting anyone else. Record the names of police personnel you speak with or who inspect your property.

4. **Prompt Notification:**
   - Notify your insurance company promptly after any damage, theft, or injury likely to result in a claim. Reporting requirements vary, but early notification accelerates the recovery process.

5. **Effective Communication:**
   - Cooperate with your insurer during the claim investigation. Follow the adjuster's directions, complete claims forms promptly, and provide any requested documents.

Prevent Denials

Proactive steps can significantly impact the success of your homeowner insurance claim! When it comes to homeowners' insurance claims, following proper procedures is essential to prevent denials and ensure approval. Here are some strategic tips:

- ➢ **Policy Understanding**:

  - ○ **Read Your Policy**: Thoroughly review your home insurance policy. Understand coverages, exclusions, and limitations. Misinterpreting your policy can lead to disappointment during the claims process.

- ➢ **Coverage Alignment**:

  - ○ **Choose Wisely**: Ensure your coverage aligns with your needs. Discuss your policy with an insurance agent to avoid surprises later. For instance, grasp the distinction between actual cash value and replacement cost coverage.

- ➢ **Appeal Process**:

  - ○ **Claim Denied? Appeal**: If your claim is denied, consider appealing. Contact your insurer, provide missing documentation, and escalate if necessary. Public adjusters or legal assistance can also be valuable allies. See Chapter

Comprehensive Property Coverage

Understanding your policy and tailoring it to your specific needs is essential! If your homeowner insurance policy excludes certain perils, here are some steps you can take to obtain coverage for those excluded risks:

- ➤ **Riders or Endorsements**:

  - ○ **More Coverage**: Consider adding specific riders or endorsements to your policy. These allow you to extend coverage for excluded perils. For example:

  - ○ **Flood Insurance**: Purchase a separate flood insurance policy to protect against flood-related damage.

  - ○ **Earthquake Insurance**: Obtain a specialized earthquake insurance policy.

  - ○ **Sewer Backup Coverage**: Add this endorsement to cover damage from sewer backups.

  - ○ **Sinkhole Coverage**: Some areas prone to sinkholes offer specific coverage.

- ➤ **Review Policy Options**:

  - ○ **HO-3 Policy**: This common type provides more comprehensive coverage for your home on an open perils basis, while personal belongings are covered on a named perils basis.

  - ○ **HO-5 Policy**: The most comprehensive option, covering both your home and belongings on an open perils basis.

  - ○ **Consult with an Agent**: Discuss your needs with an insurance agent. They can guide you on the best coverage options based on your location, property, and budget.

CHAPTER 5

....

Emergency Measure
Services

Chapter 5: Emergency Measure Services

Emergency Measure Services (EMS) are crucial for homeowners facing unexpected incidents. Swiftly securing doors, windows, and vulnerable areas prevents further damage or theft. Covering damaged roofs with tarps prevents water intrusion and protects interiors. Immediate fixes stabilize structures, prevent worsening conditions, and maintain safety. Addressing water damage promptly prevents mold growth and structural issues. Proper removal of mold ensures health safety and property preservation.

Who Pays For These Services?

In the context of homeowners insurance, EMS is for tarping roofs, drying out spaces, and temporary repairs are typically covered by the insurance carrier. These services aim to prevent further damage after a loss. However, there are policy limits for such measures. For instance, the insurer may pay up to a specified amount (e.g., $3,000 or 1% of the Coverage A limit) for reasonable emergency measures. If costs exceed this, approval from the insurer is necessary. So, while the insurance carrier pays for these services, it's essential to understand the policy terms and limits.

Secure Your Property

Securing a property is advantageous for homeowners because it provides protection against unauthorized access, acts as a deterrent to potential intruders, offers peace of mind, can lead to savings on energy bills with smart features, and may reduce insurance premiums due to decreased risk. To arrange Emergency Measure Services through an insurance carrier, homeowners should review their policy details, prepare necessary information, and contact the insurer using the provided emergency assistance number.

➤ **Secure Property:**

  ○ Protect your home from vandalism or theft during repairs by Board up broken windows, roof or secure entry points.

➤ **Instructions For Homeowners:**

  ○ Board Windows/Doors: Use plywood or secure locks.

  ○ Remove Valuables: Safeguard important items.

  ○ Notify Authorities: Report any suspicious activity.

  ○ Contact your carrier for possible Emergency Measure Services.

Tarping Roofs

EMS are crucial steps taken immediately after a loss to prevent further damage to your property such as tarping roofs. Remember, acting swiftly and documenting everything is essential for successful claims! Let's dive into detail, including examples and instructions for homeowners:

➤ **Tarping Roofs:**

  ○ If a storm damages your roof, tarp it promptly to avoid additional water damage.

➤ **Homeowner Tip #1** (If roof coverage approved)

  ○ **Your Carrier Can Help**: Ask your carrier for tarp assistance as part of your policy's conditions clause, related to Duties After Loss; prevent further damage. Normally, carriers will only coverage the expense once. Subsequent tarp replacements become the policy holder's out of pocket expense.

➤ **Homeowner Tip #2** (If roof coverage denied)

  ○ **Secure Tarp**: Use heavy-duty tarps and secure them tightly to prevent wind lift.

- o **For Repairs Only**: Use sandbags or tape.

- o **For Replacements Only**: Use nails or any means necessary to prevent further damage.

- o **Get Professional Help**: If unsure, hire a professional to tarp the roof.

<u>Temporary Repairs</u>

 Before you pay for that, here's some wisdom. Use your insurance coverage. Ensuring your property is secure is advantageous for homeowners because it guards against break-ins, further damages, and energy efficiency.

Request EMS through your insurer, one should check their policy, have your claim information ready, and use the emergency number provided by the insurance company. If you need to activate Emergency Measure Services, review your insurance policy for instructions, prepare your policy details, and call the insurer's emergency number to get the necessary assistance to protect your property promptly.

It's essential for homeowners to understand the importance of security measures and know the procedure for contacting their insurance provider for emergency services when needed.

- ➤ **<u>Homeowner Temporary Repair Tips</u>:**

  - o **Assess Damage**: Identify urgent repairs (e.g., broken windows, leaks, holes).

  - o **Basic Fixes**: Use plywood, plastic sheeting, or duct tape.

  - o **Document Repairs**: Take photos <u>BEFORE & AFTER</u>, and keep receipts.

  - o **Notify Insurer**: Inform your insurance company about temporary repairs.

Water Mitigation Services

Addressing water damage promptly and correctly (which water category) is crucial! If you have to rent or purchase equipment for self-mitigation, keep your receipts and take photos of the equipment in use, then provide the evidence to your carrier for review.

➢ **Water Mitigation Services**:

- o After a plumbing leak, roof leak, shower pan, etc., address water damage promptly to prevent mold and structural issues by means of moisture extraction, drying, and sanitizing.

➢ **Homeowners Tip**:

- o Safety First: Turn off electricity in affected areas.

- o Extract Water: Use pumps or wet/dry vacuums.

- o Dry Thoroughly: Fans, dehumidifiers, and proper ventilation.

- o Sanitize: Clean and disinfect surfaces.

- o Professional Assistance: Consider hiring experts for thorough drying. Ask your carrier for EMS assistance before hiring a 3rd-party services to minimize your Out-of-Pocket (OOP) expenses.

Mold Remediation

Following natural disasters or accidental water damage, the resulting moisture can cause mold to proliferate, presenting various health challenges during restoration efforts. When it comes to EMS, acting swiftly and understanding your policy is crucial for successful mold claims. Your carrier may provide EMS services for mold remediation, FREE of charge. Here's what you need to know, along with common policy limits:

1. **<u>Mold Remediation Basics</u>**:
   - To prevent mold growth, control moisture and dry wet materials within 24-48 hours. Remediation involves cleaning, drying, or replacing affected materials, with specific methods depending on the material type and contamination size.

   - Exposure to mold can cause health issues like itchy eyes, cough, and severe allergic responses. Mold grows in moist environments and can be found on various surfaces after water damage due to disasters.

2. **<u>Insurance Coverage for Mold</u>**:
   - Limits: Policies have limits on mold coverage. Typically ranges from $1,000 to $10,000 per occurrence.

   - Additional Coverage: You can add extra mold coverage through an endorsement.

   - Exclusions: Mold due to poor maintenance or neglect is not covered.

3. **<u>Filing a Mold Claim</u>**:
   - Prompt Reporting: Report mold damage within six months of the incident.

   - Verification: Verify if you can still make a claim for hidden mold.

   - Professional Help: Consider professional mold testing and remediation.

CHAPTER 6

Claims Process Simplified

Chapter 6: Claims Process Simplified

C ooperate with your insurer during the claim investigation and follow any directions provided by the adjuster. When you discover damage to your property, follow these critical steps for documenting the damage and preparing to file a homeowners insurance claim:

STEP 1: Report Loss & Submit Evidence

➤ **File a Police Report (if needed)**:

  o If the damage involves a crime like theft or vandalism, file a police report promptly.

  o Note down the names of any police personnel you speak with or who inspect your property.

➤ **Document the Damage**:

  o EVIDENCE! - EVIDENCE! - EVIDENCE! Take plenty photos and videos of the damage. Capture details from different angles.

  o Don't discard damaged items until the claims adjuster approves.

  o If there's been a theft, make a list of missing items and prepare photos.

  o Confirm if damages exceed your deductible.

➤ **Notify Your Insurance Company**:

  o Contact your homeowners' insurance company or agent as soon as possible.

  o Provide your policy number, name, address, phone number, and email.

○ Explain what happened and describe the extent of the property damage.

○ Jot down notes and keep track of the dates of any conversations you have with your insurance agent or adjuster (See the <u>Bonus Form #3</u>),

STEP 2: Investigation, EMS, & Decision

➤ **After Filing the Claim**:

○ **Cooperate With Your Insurer**: During the claim investigation, work closely with your insurer. Investigation can normally last up to 2 weeks, but they can take longer, especially after a natural disaster or missing documents.

○ **Request EMS**: The carrier normally does not authorize EMS without coverage. If the investigation is prolonged due to carrier investigation delays, request for their EMS to prevent further damages. If warranted, carriers may assign EMS vendors, <u>FREE</u> of charge to the insured, up to your dwelling and mold policy limits. Any excess EMS expenses will the responsibility of the homeowner.

○ **Keep All Repair Receipts**: Save all receipts and photos for any expenses and repairs you make. Damages may force you to seek temporary housing or essential (bathroom, food, etc). Contact your carrier to determine coverage.

○ **DO NOT**: <u>DO NOT</u> – BEGIN DEMOLITION or REPAIRS UNTIL CARRIER INVESTION IS COMPLETE. You have no idea what is covered versus what is. Avoid the headache.

○ **Possible Outcomes**: Under Deductible, Partial Denial, Full Denial, or Full Approval.

> ## Coverage Determination:

   o **Investigation Completed**: Once the coverage determination has been finalized, you'll be notified by your Claims Adjuster. A word of advice - Expect the worst, and hope for the best.

   o **Having Disagreements**: <u>First try to resolve them with your insurer</u>. Don't feel rushed or pushed to agree with something you aren't comfortable with. If you and the insurer still disagree about the value of the claim, check your policy for an appraisal clause. Another option is to hire a Public Adjuster (PA) or an attorney if the process becomes complex.

   o **Public Adjuster:** Hiring a public adjuster can help you navigate the claim more effectively and potentially secure a more generous claims payout for you. However, PA charge fees (typically 10%-20% of the settlement), which may be lower than attorney fees but still impact your payout. For straightforward claims, hiring a PA might not be essential.

STEP 3: Estimates, Settlement, Repairs

> ## Insurance Estimate

   o **Repair Assessment**: The insurance company will assign a Claims Adjuster will assess the property's **Replacement Cost Value** (RCV), **Actual Cash Value** (ACV), and **Depreciation**. These adjusters may be employees of the company or independent contractors.

   o **Who comes up with these numbers?!** If you're dealing with a property insurance claim, your adjuster may use a program called, Xactimate, to assess the repair costs. Xactimate is a widely used software program in the insurance industry for estimating repair costs. It helps adjusters, contractors, and insurance companies calculate the expenses associated with property damage, such as repairs after a disaster or accident. Xactimate is continually updated to reflect current pricing and industry standards.

> **Settlement Check**

- ○ **First Payment**: You'll receive a check for the **ACV** amount, minus your deductible, and possibly less **Recoverable Depreciation** (RD). This represents the current value of the damaged item.

- ○ **Minus From Settlement:** Several components are typically **subtracted** to determine the ACV settlement payout for repairs, such as Deductible, Recoverable Depreciation (RD), and Non-RD. Use the ACV payment to repair or replace the damaged property.

- ○ **Deductible**: The homeowner's deductible amount is subtracted from the total repair estimate. This is the portion the homeowner is responsible for paying out of pocket before insurance coverage kicks in.

- ○ **Recoverable Depreciation (RD)**: The depreciated value of damaged items is subtracted. Depreciation considers wear and tear over time. For example, if a roof needs replacement, the insurer accounts for its age and condition.

- ○ **Prior Payments:** Prior payments, coverage-specific, applies to supplement payments.

- ○ **Non-Covered Items**: Any repairs or replacements that fall outside the policy coverage are subtracted. For instance, if the policy excludes certain perils (e.g., flooding), those costs won't be included.

- ○ **Parties On Check**: The insurance carrier will include all policy holders on the check, for endorsement. Be sure that your insurance carrier has updated information about your mortgage holder (lien holders). Many mortgage companies have either sold existing loans to other mortgage lenders or have been acquired by larger entities. Also, if there are more the one policy holder, but one of the policy holders is now deceased, notify your carrier.

> **Hire Professional**:

- ○ **FREE QUOTES**: That ol' saying, *"If it's too good to be true… it is,"* is absolutely true. You might be encouraged or pressured to sign an "agreement" for this free estimate. Why, so the contractor can bind you to payment for time, commonly $1,000 - $2,000. DO NOT SIGN ANYTHING, unless you are certain about your decision.

- **Selecting a Contractor**: Ensure the contractor has the proper credentials. Seek multiple bids to ensure competitive pricing. Check the contractor's track record for reliability. Demand a contract that outlines the job specifics because your insurance may require an itemized repair estimate.

- **Warning Signs**: Avoid paying substantial deposits before work begins. Keep command of your insurance claim proceedings. Confirm the repair quality meets your standards before paying in full. Document all transactions and communications. Watch out for fraudulent contractors, particularly following major incidents. (See Chapter 9 for hiring).

STEP 4: Additional Damages

➤ **Additional Damges**

- **OMG – Are you kidding?!:** "*That wasn't there before!*" Or "*I didn't know!*" are normal reactions to damages caused by the loss, but where not seen during the visual inspection. Additional damages may be found after a field adjuster's inspection due to hidden issues that weren't initially visible, secondary problems arising from the original damage, oversights in the initial assessment, new damage from subsequent events, or the worsening of the initial damage over time.

o **Act Quick**: When additional damages are discovered after demolition has begun, it's important for homeowners to take a systematic approach. First, STOP EVERYTHING! Document the new damages with photographs and detailed notes. This evidence will be crucial when updating your insurance claim or discussing the situation with contractors.

STEP 5: Supplement Claim

➢ **Getting Started – Again**

o **Settlement Payment, Not Enough**: Don't worry. You can file a supplement claim for any additional claim-related expenses for subsequent payments until the insurance carrier issues a final settlement.

o **Provide Supporting Evidence**: Contact your insurance company to report the additional damages, as a supplemental claim. They may need to reassess your claim and adjust the coverage accordingly. If the damages are extensive, consider consulting a structural engineer to ensure the safety and integrity of your home. Remember, addressing these issues promptly can prevent further damage and may help expedite the repair process.

➢ **Another Payment**

o **Subsequent Payments**: If the initial settlement was not enough, don't worry. You can file a supplement claim for any additional claim-related expenses for subsequent payments until the insurance carrier issues a final settlement.

o After the new evidence has been reviewed by the carrier and approved. A supplement settlement amount will be issued accordingly, just as the initial settlement payment.

STEP 6: Request Your RD & OL

> ### Recoverable Depreciation (RD)

  - **All Done**: Check your initial estimate or supplemental estimate for and RD. Your carrier may withhold RD until after proof of repairs have been completed, and proof has been provided. Once the carrier confirms the repairs are completed, the remaining RD amount will be released accordingly, just as previous settlement payments.

> ### Ordinance And Law (O&L)

  - **Building Requirement**: O&L coverage in a property claim addresses the extra expenses incurred (you pay 1st) to bring a damaged home up to the latest building and safety standards required by local laws during the repair process. It's a safeguard against the unforeseen costs that can arise due to evolving construction regulations.

  - **Example**: Should a homeowner's roof be damaged, O&L coverage may provide financial assistance for the additional costs incurred to ensure the roof's reconstruction adheres to the latest building regulations. This could involve fitting enhanced shingles, securing the structure with hurricane straps, or using roofing nails of a regulated size that were not stipulated at the time of the original construction.

  - **Pay Up**: Once the carrier confirms the repairs are completed, the remaining RD amount will be released accordingly, just as previous settlement payments.

STEP 7: Follow-Up As Necessary

➤ **Loose-Ends**

- **Unfinished Business**: It's crucial for homeowners to actively follow up on their insurance policy claim when maximizing the settlement. By staying engaged with the insurance company, homeowners can provide additional documentation, clarify details, and address any discrepancies that may arise.

- **Timely Follow-Ups**: Expedites the claims process, allowing for quicker repairs and reimbursement. Moreover, it allows home-owners to stay informed about their claim status and any potential changes in coverage.

CHAPTER 7

Common Denial Reasons

Chapter 7: Common Denial Reasons

Homeowners insurance policies have specific exclusions, conditions, or events that **are not** covered by the insurance company. Policy specifics can vary, so always review your policy and consider additional coverage if needed. Here are some common H03 exclusions:

1. **Flooding**: Homeowners insurance does **not** cover water damage caused by natural flooding, rain, sewer line or sump pump backups, or water that seeps up from the ground and damages your home's foundation. Burst pipes or a defunct water heater would be covered, though.

2. **Earth Movements**: This refers to damage caused by earthquakes, land shock waves, volcanic eruptions, landslides, mudslides, subsidence, sinkholes, and other shifting of the earth. However, fire or explosion damage resulting from earth movement is covered.

3. **Pest Infestations**: Damage caused by animals (such as rats, termites, bees, bats, or bed bugs) is generally not covered, except under rare circumstances.

4. **Mold or Wet Rot**: Mold-related damage is often excluded unless it results from a covered peril (like a burst pipe).

5. **Certain Dog Breeds**: Some policies exclude liability coverage for specific dog breeds with a history of aggression.

6. **Wear and Tear or Neglect**: Damage due to poor maintenance or neglect is typically not covered.

7. **Power Surges Caused by Utility Companies**: While power surges from other sources may be covered, those caused by utility companies are often excluded.

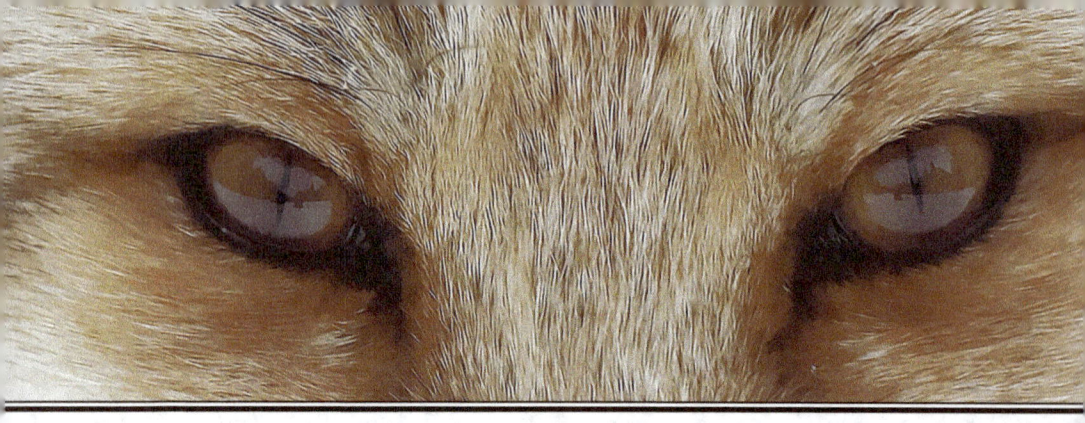

CHAPTER 8

Negotiation Strategies

Chapter 8: Negotiation Strategies

When negotiating a property insurance claim, homeowners can employ several effective negotiation strategies to maximize their settlement. Remember that negotiation is a process, and persistence pays off. Stay informed, advocate for your rights, and seek professional assistance if needed. Here are some tips:

➢ **Understand Your Policy:**

  ○ Begin by thoroughly reviewing your insurance policy. Understand the coverage limits, deductibles, and exclusions. This knowledge will empower you during negotiations.

  ○ **Document Everything:**

    1. Keep detailed records of the entire claims process. Document conversations with insurance representatives, adjusters, and contractors.

    2. Take photos or videos of the damage to support your claim. Visual evidence can be compelling.

➢ **Be Prepared:**

  ○ Before negotiating, research the fair market value of the repairs or replacements needed. Obtain estimates from contractors.

  ○ Be ready to present evidence of the actual cost of repairs or replacement.

➢ **Stay Calm and Professional:**

  ○ Approach negotiations with a calm demeanor. Avoid becoming confrontational or emotional.

  ○ Be respectful and professional in all interactions.

- ➢ **<u>Start High</u>:**

  - ○ When making your initial claim, ask for a higher amount than you expect to receive. This gives you room to negotiate downward.

  - ○ Justify your requested amount with evidence (e.g., repair estimates).

- ➢ **<u>Leverage Licensed Professionals</u>:**

  - ○ Consider hiring a public adjuster. They work on your behalf and have experience negotiating with insurance companies.

  - ○ Public adjusters can help you navigate complex claims and ensure you receive a fair settlement.

- ➢ **<u>Consider Mediation or Appraisal</u>:**

  - ○ If negotiations stall, suggest mediation or appraisal. Mediation involves a neutral third-party facilitating negotiation discussions.

  - ○ Appraisal involves an independent appraiser assessing the claim value.

  - ○ Contact the insurance company and propose mediation as a way to resolve disagreements.

  - ○ **Benefits**:

    1. Faster resolution than going to court.
    2. Confidential and less adversarial.
    3. Opportunity to express your concerns and find common ground.

I Was Denied – Do I appeal?!

When your homeowners' insurance claim is denied, don't give up. Review the denial letter carefully. It's essential to review your policy, gather evidence, and communicate with your insurer during the appeal process. Understanding the pros and cons of appealing the decision isn't a bad idea either.

- ➤ **Pros of Appealing a Denied Claim**:

    - ○ **Higher Payout**: An appeal could result in a more favorable settlement if you believe the denial was incorrect.

    - ○ **Additional Documentation**: You can present new evidence or clarify existing information to strengthen your case.

    - ○ **Professional Assistance**: Consider hiring an independent appraiser or public adjuster to advocate for your claim.

- ➤ **Cons of Appealing**:

    - ○ **Time and Effort**: Appeals take time and effort, and there's no guarantee of success.

    - ○ **Legal Costs**: If the appeal fails, legal fees may be incurred if you decide to pursue further action.

    - ○ **Strained Relationship**: The appeal process can strain your relationship with the insurer.

CHAPTER 9

Hiring Contractors

Chapter 9: Hiring Contractors

The types of licenses needed for repairing or building a residential building vary by state. The letters associated with different residential contractor licenses can vary by state. Check your state's specific requirements and obtain the necessary licenses before undertaking any residential construction work! Here's a general overview:

General Contractor License

➤ **License by Category:**

   ○ **Certified General Contractor (CGC):** Valid statewide for various construction projects.

   ○ **Registered General Contractor (RGC):** Limited to specific local jurisdictions.

   ○ **Examples of states requiring this license:** Alabama, California, Florida, Georgia, and Texas.

➤ **Required For**: Required in most states for constructing, altering, repairing, or demolishing any building or structure (commercial, industrial, or residential).

Specialty Contractor License

➤ **License by Category**:

   ○ Qualifying Builder (QB): For general residential construction.

   ○ Qualifying Remodeler (QR): Focused on remodeling work.

   ○ Qualifying Roofer (QR): Specializing in roofing projects.

> **Required For:**

  o Examples: Electricians, plumbers, and HVAC technicians specialized work within a residential building.

Residential Contractor License

> **License by Category:**

  o **Residential Contractor (RC):** Homebuilders, remodelers, and repair contractors covers residential building, repair, and remodeling;
  Focusing on residential properties (usually three stories or fewer).

Choosing A Contractor

Thorough research and clear communication are key to successful property repairs and hiring reliable contractors! Remember, a quote is not a contract, and homeowners should be cautious about signing anything until they're ready to commit to a specific contractor. Let's cover some essential tips for each of these areas:

1. **Getting a Residential Property Repair Quote:**
   - **Multiple Bids:** Obtain quotes from at least three different contrac-
     tors. This helps you understand the average cost and avoid over-
     paying.

   - **Detailed Estimates:** Ask for a written estimate that includes proj-
     ect details, materials, completion date, and price. Compare these
     carefully.

   - **Quality Over Price:** Don't automatically choose the lowest bidder.
     Consider the quality of work and ask for explanations if estimates
     vary significantly.

2. **Hiring a Contractor:**
   - **Recommendations:** Start by asking friends and family for contrac-
     tor recommendations. Trustworthy referrals are valuable.

- **Check Credentials**: Verify that contractors are licensed and insured. Contact your state or county government to confirm their license status.

- **Research Online**: Read customer reviews and search online for any complaints or scams associated with the contractor.

- **Face-to-Face Meeting**: Meet potential contractors in person to assess communication and compatibility. Trust your instincts.

3. **Avoiding Scams**:

   - **Door-to-Door Contractors**: Be cautious of contractors who knock on your door unexpectedly. Scammers often use this tactic.

   - **Immediate Pressure**: Scammers may pressure you for an immediate decision. Take your time and don't rush into agreements.

   - **Upfront Payments**: Avoid contractors who demand full payment upfront or only accept cash. Reputable contractors follow standard payment schedules.

   - **Inspect Their Work**: Visit a current job site to see how the contractor operates. Is the site neat, safe, and well-managed?

Checking Contractor License

Verify credentials before hiring any contractor for your home improvement projects! To find licensed contractors in your state, follow these steps:

1. **Online Database**:

   o **Check Your State's Website:** Visit your state's official website or licensing board.

   o **Search for Licensed Contractors:** Look for an online database of licensed professionals.

   o **Enter Contractor Details:** Enter the contractor's name, company name, or license number to verify their license status.

2. **State-Specific Resources**:
   - ○ **Other States**: Each state has its own licensing board or agency. Search for your state's specific resources.

Getting A FREEEE Estimate. Right?

A repair quote is not a contract, and homeowners should be cautious about signing anything until they're ready to commit to a specific contractor. When a contractor provides a "**free quote**," it **SHOULD NOT** **require a signature** from the homeowner. It's essential to have clear contract language to define any termination fees and ensure both parties understand their obligations. Here's why:

1. **Informal Nature of Quotes**:
   - A quote is an initial estimate of the project cost. It's not a legally binding contract.

   - Homeowners often receive multiple free quotes before making a decision.

2. **Consequences of Signing a "FREE" Quote**:
   - **Binding Agreement:** If you sign a quote, it could be interpreted as a contract.

   - **Legal Obligations:** You might unintentionally commit to hiring that contractor, even if you find a better offer later.

   - **Payment Disputes:** If issues arise, the signed quote may limit your ability to dispute charges.

   - Contractors often include a custom termination fee clause in their contracts to address situations where the contract is terminated. This clause allows the homeowner to terminate the contract without cause. However, the contractor may be entitled to compensation for NO work performed or costs incurred. This fee can range upwards of $3,000.

3. **Best Practices**:

- **Get Multiple Quotes**: Compare quotes without signing anything.

- **Formal Contracts**: When you decide on a contractor, a formal written contract should outline all terms, costs, and project details.

- **Avoid Pressure**: Don't feel pressured to sign immediately. Take your time to make an informed choice.

Watch Out! – Read The Contract!

Homeowners sometimes sign contracts with contractors prematurely due to several common mistakes. Let's explore these pitfalls and their consequences:

➢ **Pressure to Make a Quick Decision**:

- o Mistake: Homeowners may feel pressured by contractors who insist on an immediate commitment.

- o Consequence: Rushed decisions can lead to hiring an unqualified or unreliable contractor.

➢ **Paying in Full Upfront**:

- o Mistake: Some homeowners pay the entire project cost upfront, assuming it's standard practice.

- o Consequence: Paying in full before work begins risks losing leverage if issues arise during the project.

➢ **Lack of Clear Instructions**:

- o Mistake: Homeowners assume contractors understand their vision without providing explicit instructions.

- o Consequence: Misunderstandings and mistakes can occur, resulting in unsatisfactory work.

➢ **Not Checking Credentials**:

- o Mistake: Failing to verify a contractor's license and insurance.

- o Consequence: Hiring an unlicensed or uninsured contractor risks poor workmanship and potential legal issues.

➢ **Ignoring Reviews and Recommendations**:

- o Mistake: Disregarding feedback from trusted sources or online reviews.

- o Consequence: Missing valuable insights about a contractor's reputation and reliability.

➢ **Skipping Detailed Contracts**:

- o Mistake: Not having a written contract that outlines project details, payment terms, and timelines.

- o Consequence: Disputes can arise due to unclear expectations or unmet promises.

Reporting Contractors

Verify contractor credentials and research contractors thoroughly before hiring them for any home improvement projects! To report licensed contractors, you can take the following steps:

1. **National Association of State Contractors Licensing Agencies (NA-SCLA)**:

- o Visit the NASCLA website.

- o NASCLA provides resources related to construction licensing, including information on state licensing agencies and application requirements.

- o Unfortunately, there isn't a single national phone number for reporting contractors, as each state manages its licensing and enforcement.

2. **State and Local Resources**:
   - Check with Your State or County Government: Confirm a contractor's license by contacting your state or county government. They can verify a contractor's credentials.

   - Ask for Proof of Insurance: Always ask contractors for proof of insurance.

   - Get Recommendations: Seek recommendations from trusted sources, such as friends, family, or local Home Builders Associations.

   - Check with the Better Business Bureau: Look up contractors to see if there are any consumer complaints lodged against them.

CHAPTER 10

Supplement Claim

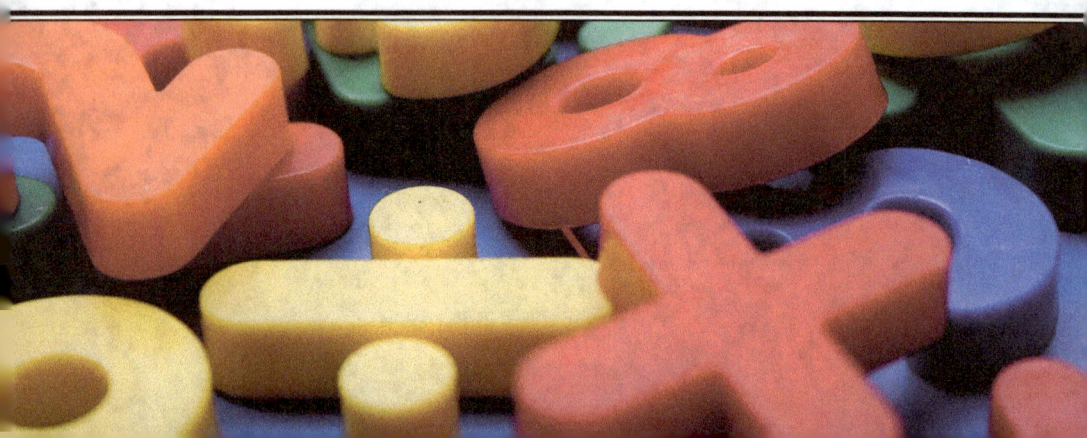

Chapter 10: Supplement Claim

Consult your insurance provider for specific details related to a supplemental claim in your policy! Let's delve into the details of supplement claims:

➤ **Definition**:

   ○ Supplemental claims occur when the homeowner will contact their carrier, as a follow-up, to submit additional claim-related documents, after the initial assessment, to account for any overlooked or underestimated costs.

➤ **Benefit**:

   ○ Supplemental claims help ensure that you receive the full maximized coverage you're entitled to. When unexpected damages or expenses arise, these claims bridge the gap between the initial estimate and the actual costs.

➤ **Avoiding Out-of-Pocket Costs**:

   ○ By filing a supplemental claim, you can avoid paying for unforeseen expenses out of your own pocket. It helps prevent financial strain due to unexpected bills.

Determining Supplement Eligibility

For a Supplemental Property Claim, to assess whether your property claim qualifies for a supplemental claim, consider the following factors:

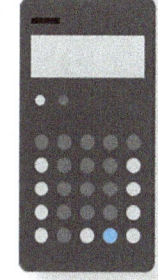

1. **Initial Claim**: First, ensure that you've already filed an initial property claim. A supplemental claim typically follows an initial claim, for Recoverable Deprecation, Ordinance & Law, or additional expenses related to

Like, Kind, & Quality (LKQ) such as contractor invoices, temporary living (food, hotel), loss of rental income.

2. **Changed Circumstances**: Supplemental claims are appropriate when there have been significant changes or under-estimated repairs by carrier, since the initial claim.

3. **These changes might include:**

   o **New Evidence**: If you have additional evidence related to your property damage or loss.

   o **Re-evaluation**: If you believe the initial assessment was incomplete or inaccurate. This is usually warranted only with proof of damages. So be prepared.

   o **Unforeseen Damage**: If you discover additional damages, after the initial claim, not evident during the initial visual inspection by the Field Adjuster.

4. **Timeliness**: File your supplemental claim promptly. Delays may affect eligibility.

5. **Consult Professionals**: Seek advice from your insurance company, a public adjuster, or a legal professional. They can guide you based on your specific circumstances.

Self-Repair Vs Contractor

Choosing between Do-It-Yourself (DIY) repairs and professional services involves considering factors like cost, expertise, and time. Self-repair can be less expensive but might lead to subpar results and take more time. Professional contractors offer skill and efficiency but at a higher price and with the potential difficulty of finding a trustworthy service provider.

➢ **Self-Repairs**: If you plan to do the repairs yourself, message your adjuster and submit supporting documents (photos and an itemized estimate) for review. Tackling repairs yourself can be lighter on the wallet and allows you to manage the project directly. The main risks include the possibility of not fixing the issue properly and the significant amount of time it might take.

➤ **Exceeding the Estimate**: If the contractor's estimates or repairs end up costing more than the carrier's repair estimate, you might be responsible for the excess amount, not covered. Always communicate with your adjuster before starting repairs.

➤ Refer to <u>Chapter 9: Hiring Contractors</u>, for the type of skilled-trade needed for repair estimates.

Get Your Recoverable Depreciation

Depreciation is based on the age and condition of the damaged item. Essentially, it accounts for the wear and tear over time. Here are the steps to take for recovering your **Recoverable Depreciation (RD)**:

1. **Submit Documentation**: After repairing or replacing the damages, <u>submit receipts</u>, <u>photos of repairs</u>, <u>proof of payment</u>, <u>estimates/invoices</u>, and relevant paperwork to your insurer, as a Supplement Claim.

2. **Itemization**: An itemized estimate helps your adjuster review your claim more quickly. It's also necessary to show all damaged materials. Make sure your estimate is detailed and itemized.

3. **Second Payment**: Your insurer will then issue a second payment for the **recoverable depreciation** amount.

How To Get Remaining Funds

The supplement process may vary slightly depending on your specific carrier and policy. Always consult with your insurance provider for accurate guidance tailored to your situation. When it comes to starting a supplement claim with your homeowners' insurance carrier, follow these steps:

1. **Contact Your Insurance Company**: Reach out to your insurance company promptly. Let them know that you need to file a supplement claim.

2. **Provide Documentation**: Gather all necessary documentation, including receipts and invoices for materials and labor. This evidence will support your claim. Provide the documentation to your insurance company. You can do this through their preferred method (e.g., online portal or email).

Remember, ABOVE ALL, each case is unique, and eligibility depends on the specifics of your property claim. Contact your insurance provider for a personalized guidance.

CHAPTER 11

....

ANYTHING ELSE?

Chapter 11: Anything Else?

Homeowners insurance is essential for protecting assets and satisfying mortgage lenders. It covers various perils such as plumbing leaks, wind, fire, theft, vandalism, and natural disasters. Understanding the claim process, premiums, and deductibles is crucial. The roles in the insurance claim process include insurance carriers who underwrite and provide coverage, insurance agents who sell policies, field and desk adjusters who assess damages, public adjusters who represent the insured, and claims attorneys who handle disputes.

Key components of property insurance policies include coverage limits, deductibles, and exclusions. It's important to clarify these aspects to understand what is covered and what isn't. Coverage conditions and exclusions need to be reviewed annually. Matching coverage and understanding the statute of limitations are also critical to ensure that claims are filed timely and accurately.

Common claims include structural damage, wind and hail damage, fire and lightning damage, water damage, mold damage, and theft-related damage. Each type of damage requires specific skilled trades for assessment and repair. For instance, engineers assess structural damage, while plumbers and water damage restoration experts handle water-related issues. Promptly involving the appropriate professionals is essential for accurate repair estimates and successful claims.

Timely claim submission and effective documentation are vital for a smooth claims process. Homeowners should notify their insurer immediately after a loss, pay premiums on time, understand their policy, mitigate damage, and document everything thoroughly. Proper documentation includes photos, receipts, and communication records. Proactive steps like these prevent denials and ensure claims are processed efficiently.

Emergency Measure Services (EMS) include securing doors and windows, tarping roofs, and making temporary repairs to prevent further damage. These services are typically covered by insurance carriers within policy limits. Homeowners should review their policy details and contact their insurer for emergency assistance. Proper EMS can prevent additional damage and stabilize structures, ensuring safety and preserving property.

The claims process involves several steps: reporting the loss and submitting evidence, cooperating with the insurer during the investigation, receiving EMS, getting estimates, and settling the claim. Additional damages discovered later can be addressed through supplemental claims. It's important to follow up as necessary and request recoverable depreciation and ordinance or law coverage when applicable. Understanding this process helps homeowners navigate claims more effectively and ensures they receive fair compensation.

Matthew

7: 24 - 25

" *Whoever hears these teachings of mine and obeys them is like a wise man who built his house on rock.*

It rained hard, the floods came, and the winds blew and beat against that house. But it did not fall because it was built on rock.

Claims can be denied for various reasons, such as policy exclusions, failure to maintain the property, or not providing sufficient documentation. Homeowners should thoroughly understand their policy, document all damages and repairs, and communicate effectively with their insurer to avoid denials. If a claim is denied, homeowners can appeal by providing additional documentation and, if necessary, seeking professional assistance.

Effective negotiation strategies include understanding the policy, documenting everything, being prepared with repair estimates, staying calm and professional, and starting high in negotiations. Homeowners can leverage licensed professionals like public adjusters and consider mediation or appraisal if negotiations stall. Appealing a denied claim can result in a higher payout, but it requires time and effort. Understanding the pros and cons of appealing helps homeowners make informed decisions.

Choosing the right contractor is crucial for successful property repairs. Homeowners should obtain multiple bids, verify contractor credentials, check online reviews, and avoid scams. Contracts should outline job specifics, and homeowners should avoid paying substantial deposits upfront. Thorough research and clear communication are key to hiring reliable contractors and ensuring quality repairs.

Supplemental claims are necessary when initial settlement payments are insufficient to cover all damages. Homeowners should document additional damages and provide supporting evidence to their insurer. Filing a supplement claim involves contacting the insurance company, submitting necessary documentation, and requesting further payments. Understanding the process for recovering recoverable depreciation and ordinance or law coverage ensures homeowners receive the funds needed for complete repairs.

Homeowners insurance is a vital tool for protecting property and assets. Understanding the policy, promptly reporting claims, effectively documenting damages, and following the claims process can significantly impact the success of insurance claims. Homeowners should be proactive, informed, and prepared to negotiate or appeal if necessary, ensuring they receive fair compensation for covered damages. By following the guidelines in this book, you ARE going to maximize your settlement.

May God bless you with knowledge, understanding, and wisdom, forever and ever, amen.

The End.

EXTRA BONUSES

....

EXACTLY WHAT'S NEEDED

BONUS #1: Property Insurance Definitions

Actual Cost Value (ACV)	Your 1st settlement amount, minus your deductible, and possibly less Recoverable Depreciation (RD).
Deductible	This is the portion the homeowner is responsible for paying out of pocket. The homeowner's deductible amount is subtracted from the total repair estimate.
Dwelling	Your home and attached structures (carports, lanais, pool cage, etc).
Emergency Measure Services (EMS)	EMS, similar to a 1st-responder, providing board-up water mitigation, mold inspection & remediation, demolition, etc.
Homeowners Insurance	Provides financial protection for your home and belongings. It covers losses due to events like plumbing leaks, wind, fire, theft, vandalism, or natural disasters.
Loss of Use (ALE)	Assisted Living Expense (ALE), if your home becomes uninhabitable due to a covered disaster, this coverage helps pay for temporary living expenses (like hotel costs) while your home is being repaired.
Peril	A specific risk or reason for a loss. Some policies cover all perils except ones specifically excluded. At the other extreme are policies that cover only the perils named in the policy.
Personal Liability (PL)	Financial loss if you are sued and found legally responsible for injuries or damages to someone else.
Personal Property	The value of your possessions, including furniture, electronics, appliances and clothing, damaged or lost even when they aren't on your property
Ordinance and Law (OL)	coverage to bring a damaged home up to the latest local building and safety standards required by local laws during the repair process.
Other Structure	Pays for damage to fences, tool sheds, freestanding garages, guest cottages and other structures not attached to your house.
Recoverable Depreciation (RD)	Depreciation is based on the age and condition of the damaged item, accounting for the wear and tear over time. The difference between RCV and ACV is called Recoverable Depreciation.
Settlement	A sum of money paid as compensation for repairs minus RD, Deductible, Prior pay, and Non-RD.
Supplement Claim	Occurs when initial estimates fall short, ensuring full coverage for unforeseen damages or expenses.

BONUS #2: Homeowner's Claim Flowchart

After all that reading, use this book as your reference when filing a claim, but for those who would like a visual, this is for you. Below is a visual of a homeowner's claim process in 7 steps, from the beginning to the end.

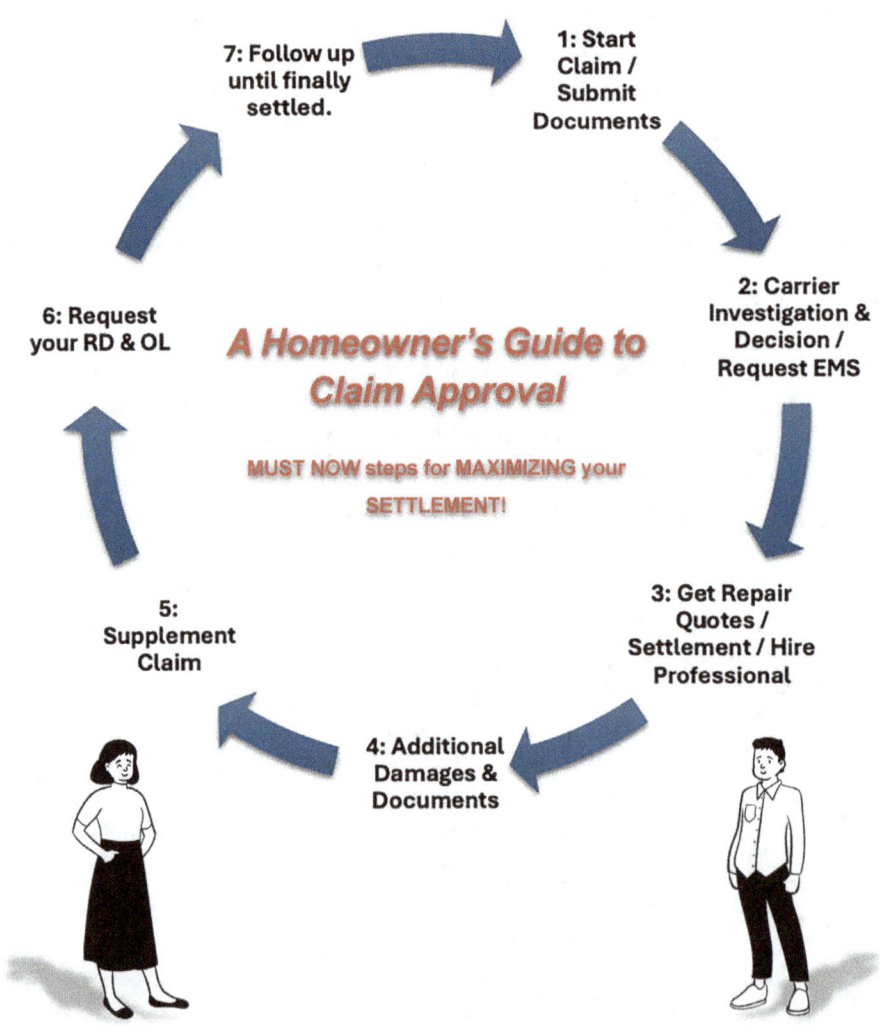

BONUS #3: Homeowner's Claim Tracker

Here's a basic template for a homeowners claim tracker form that you can use as a starting point. Feel free to customize it further based on your specific needs:

Claim Details

- Date of Incident: _____
- Description of Incident: _____
- Date Claim Reported: _____
- Police Report Number (if applicable): _____

Insurance Information

- Insurance Company: _____
- Phone # & Email: _____
- Policy Number: _____
- Sale's Agent Name and POC: _____

Claim Tracking

- Claim Number: _____
- Adjuster's Name and POC: _____
- Dwelling Settlement Amount: _____
- Other Structure Settlement Amount: _____
- Personal Property Settlement Amount: _____

3rd-Party Contractor Repair Estimates

- 1st Contractor Name and POC: _____
- Description of Repairs: _____
- License # and Estimate for Repairs: _____
- 2nd Contractor Name and POC: _____
- Description of Temporary Repairs: _____
- License # and Estimate for Repairs: _____

BONUS #4: Ways To Lower Premiums

Here are some improvement ideas that not only enhance safety but also contribute to potential cost savings. Always check with your insurance provider for specific details and discounts related to home upgrades.

---

1. **Replace Your Roof**: Upgrading to a new roof can significantly impact insurance rates. For example, replacing an older roof with a newly constructed one can lead to substantial savings. Consider fire- or wind-resistant roofing materials for additional discounts.

2. **Install Storm-Resistant Windows**: Impact-resistant windows reduce the risk of damage from wind, hail, and water, which are common reasons for insurance claims. These storm-resistant starter kits can lead to cost savings on premiums.

3. **Add a Security System**: Installing deadbolts, fire alarms, or a monitored security system can result in discounts on homeowners' insurance. Opt for central station devices that directly alert emergency services or try self-monitoring security systems for homes.

4. **Upgrade Home Utility Systems**: Improving electrical, smart thermostat, smart space-heaters, portable smart A/C units, and smart plumbing systems reduces the risk of accidental fires and water damage. Insurers may offer premium reductions for safer home systems.

5. **Enhance Home Safety Features**: Consider adding smart smoke detectors, fire extinguishers, and smart carbon monoxide detectors. These safety features demonstrate responsible home maintenance and may lead to insurance discounts.

6. **Choose Wind-Resistant Construction**: If you live in an area prone to wind-related damage, opt for wind-resistant construction materials. Insurers often reward such choices with lower premiums.

7. **Storm-related Preparation**: Be prepared, before a natural disaster, with essential first-aid supplies like thermal blankets, canteens, bandages, gauze, tweezers, and safety pins. Also, flood preparation is becoming more of a necessity. Inflatable boats can help danger due to unexpected flood. Solar-power & wind-power generators are available until power is restored.

BONUS #5: <u>Valuable Homeowner Resources</u>

Being informed, staying informed, and being prepared empowers homeowners to make better decisions and make a significant difference to protect their investments!

➤ **Understanding Homeowners Insurance:**

- ○ **The National Association of Insurance Commissioners** (NAIC) provides a comprehensive guide on homeowners insurance. Go to: https:// naic.org/sites/default/files/publication-hoi-pp-consumer-homeowners.pdf.

- ○ **Consumer Reports** is an independent, nonprofit member organization that works side by side with consumers for truth, transparency, and fairness in the marketplace. View @ https://www.consumerreports.org/money/homeowners-insurance/buying-guide/

- ○ The mission of **Environmental Protection Agency** (EPA) is to protect human health and the environment - today and every day. Go to https://www.epa.gov.

➤ **Federal Insurance Resources:**

- ○ Individuals and Households Program (IHP) provides financial and direct services to eligible individuals and households affected by disasters. It covers uninsured or under-insured necessary expenses and serious needs.

- ○ The **National Oceanic and Atmospheric Administration (NOAA) Sea Grant programs developed** Homeowner's Handbook to Prepare for Natural Disasters for individual states. This handbook offers actionable information on how natural disasters (such as hurricanes, floods, and tornadoes) will likely affect residents..

- ○ The Federal Emergency Management Agency (FEMA) plays a crucial role in supporting citizens and emergency personnel. FEMA can help with Disaster Assistance, Preparedness and Response, and Equity and Climate Resilience.

- ○ The National Flood Insurance Program (NFIP) provides insurance to property owners, renters, and businesses to help reduce the socio-economic impact of floods.